KB245436

주토피아2, 5년 후 나에게 : Q&A a day

초판 1쇄 펴낸 날 2026년 1월 1일 펴낸곳 더모던
전화 02)3141-4421 팩스 0505-333-4428 등록 2012년 3월 16일(제 313-2012-81호)
주소 서울시 마포구 성미산로32길 12, 2층 (우 03983) E-mail sanhonjinju@naver.com
카페 cafe.naver.com/mirbookcompany 인스타그램 www.instagram.com/mirbooks

HELLO
CLARK
GRIZZLY
HELLO
HELLO

NC BELL
F R SERVICE

Disney
ZOOTOPIA
2
1
January

1

What are three things you really want to accomplish this year?
올해 꼭 이루고 싶은 세 가지를 말해줄래?

20

20

20

20

20

How do you feel when you wake up in the morning?

아침에 일어나면 어떤 기분이야?

20

20

20

20

20

3

What was the best part of your day?
오늘 하루 중에 가장 기분이 좋았던 일은 뭐야?

20

20

20

20

20

4

If you were to pick a new hobby, what would be ideal for you?

새로운 취미를 가진다면 어떤 게 좋을까?

20

20

20

20

20

Do you have any bedtime habits?
잠자기 전에 하는 너만의 습관이 있니?

20

20

20

20

20

Who are you most interested in these days?

요즘 네가 가장 관심 있는 사람은 누구야?

20

20

20

20

20

What kind of music are you listening to on repeat lately?

최근에 계속 반복해서 듣는 음악은 어떤 거야?

20

20

20

20

20

If anyone suddenly came to your mind today,
write their names down.
오늘 갑자기 떠오른 사람들이 있다면 모두 적어보자.

20

20

20

20

20

Where do you want to go now?

지금 어디로 떠나고 싶어?

20

20

20

20

20

What's the word you said the most when talking to people today?

오늘 사람들과 만나면서 가장 많이 쓴 말은 뭐야?

20

20

20

20

20

11

What do you usually talk about at lunch with
your friends or co-workers?

친구나 동료들과 점심시간에 나누는 대화는 주로 어떤 거야?

20

20

20

20

20

When something good happens, is there someone
whose voice you want to hear first?

좋은 일이 있을 때 가장 먼저 목소리를 듣고 싶은 사람이 있어?

20

20

20

20

20

13

Is there anyone you want to hug when you're happy?

기쁠 때 꼭 끌어안고 싶은 사람이 있어?

20

20

20

20

20

What do you want right now?

지금 가장 갖고 싶은 것은 뭐야?

20

20

20

20

20

15

What is your favorite movie? Why?

너의 인생 영화는 뭐야? 그 이유는?

20

20

20

20

20

What is your favorite book? Why?

너의 인생 책은 뭐야? 그 이유는?

20

20

20

20

20

17

What is the best thing you've bought in the past two months?

최근 두 달 동안 산 물건 중에서 가장 마음에 든 것은?

20

20

20

20

20

What does 'home' mean to you?

'집'이란 너에게 어떤 의미야?

20

20

20

20

20

19

What is your favorite food these days?

요즘 네가 가장 즐겨 먹는 음식은?

20

20

20

20

20

What would you most like to hear before you go to bed tonight?

오늘 밤 잠들기 전에 꼭 듣고 싶은 말은 뭐야?

20

20

20

20

20

Do you have a comfort food of your own?

너만의 힐링 푸드는?

20

20

20

20

20

Sum up your TODAY in three words.

'오늘'을 세 단어로 정리해보면?

20

20

20

20

20

23

What city do you want to visit the most?

가장 가보고 싶은 도시는 어디야?

20

20

20

20

20

What kind of person do you want to be remembered as?

넌 어떤 사람으로 기억되고 싶어?

20

20

20

20

20

25

Is there a strength you have that you'd like to let shine
even more this year?

네가 가진 장점 중 올해 더 빛나게 하고 싶은 것이 있어?

20

20

20

20

20

Who spent the most time with you in a week?

일주일 동안 너랑 가장 많은 시간을 보낸 사람은 누구야?

20

20

20

20

20

27

What was your most grateful thing today?

오늘 하루, 가장 감사했던 일은?

20

20

20

20

20

Can you tell me the most memorable sentence
in the last book you read?

마지막으로 읽은 책 속에서 가장 기억에 남는 문장을 알려줄래?

20

20

20

20

20

Is there anyone you trust or depend on?

네가 믿고 의지하는 사람이 있어?

20

20

20

20

20

What city do you want to live in a month?

'한 달 살기'를 하고 싶은 도시는 어디야?

20

20

20

20

20

Who's the person you feel most about these days?
최근 가장 마음이 쓰이는 사람은 누구야?

20

20

20

20

20

Disney
ZOOTOPIA
2
February

1

Describe your favorite sky!

가장 좋아하는 하늘을 묘사해줘!

20

20

20

20

20

How do you relieve stress?

스트레스를 해소하는 너만의 방법은?

20

20

20

20

20

3

Tell me your plans for tomorrow.
내일의 계획을 들려줘.

20

20

20

20

20

What has made you the saddest lately?

최근에 가장 너를 슬프게 했던 일은 뭐야?

20

20

20

20

20

5

Where do you feel most comfortable?

네가 가장 편안함을 느끼는 장소는 어디야?

20

20

20

20

20

What kind of life do you want to live?

어떤 삶을 살고 싶어?

20

20

20

20

20

7

What color do you like the most? Why?

가장 좋아하는 색은 뭐야? 이유는?

20

20

20

20

20

When do you concentrate the best during the day?

하루 중에 가장 집중이 잘 되는 시간은 언제야?

20

20

20

20

20

9

Which day in the past week did you feel the healthiest?

최근 일주일 중에 가장 컨디션이 좋은 요일이 언제였어?

20

20

20

20

20

Can you describe the most memorable scene of today?

오늘 하루 중 가장 기억에 남는 장면이 있다면 묘사해줄래?

20

20

20

20

20

11

Which color do you think best represents you?

너를 가장 잘 표현하는 색깔이 뭐라고 생각해?

20

20

20

20

20

Have you ever overcome a fear and taken on a challenge?

두려움을 극복하고 뭔가에 도전한 일이 있어?

20

20

20

20

20

13

What's your current profile picture?

지금 프로필 사진은 어떤 거야?

20

20

20

20

20

Did you give chocolate to someone today?
What do they mean to you?

오늘 누군가에게 초콜릿을 선물했어?
그 사람은 너에게 어떤 의미야?

20

20

20

20

20

15

What are you preparing for tomorrow to make it
better than today?

지금보다 나은 내일을 위해서 어떤 일을 준비 중에 있니?

20

20

20

20

20

Is there a moment in your life that you want to go back to?

지금까지의 인생에서 돌아가고 싶은 순간이 있어?

20

20

20

20

20

17

What is the greatest driving force in your life?

네 삶의 원동력은 뭐야?

20

20

20

20

20

18

Do you love yourself?

넌, 네 자신을 사랑하니?

20

20

20

20

20

19

Who do you envy the most right now?

네가 지금 가장 부러워하는 대상은 누구야?

20

20

20

20

20

Do you think effort can change things?

노력이 상황을 바꿀 수 있다고 생각해?

20

20

20

20

20

21

What is the most recent thing that felt new to you?

최근에 겪은 가장 새로웠던 일은?

20

20

20

20

20

What kind of love do you want in your life from now on?

앞으로 어떤 사랑을 하고 싶어?

20

20

20

20

20

23

What do you want to hear the most from someone you love?

사랑하는 사람에게 가장 듣고 싶은 말이 뭐야?

20

20

20

20

20

What do you think makes a true friend?

네가 생각하는 참다운 친구는 어떤 사람이야?

20

20

20

20

20

25

How do you want others to see you?

다른 사람들 눈에 어떻게 보이고 싶어?

20

20

20

20

20

What is your biggest weakness?

너의 가장 큰 단점은 뭐라고 생각해?

20

20

20

20

20

27

What is your greatest strength?

너의 가장 큰 장점은 어떤 거야?

20

20

20

20

20

Do you have any personal jinxes or superstitions?

너만의 징크스가 있다면 뭘까?

20

20

20

20

20

29

What did you do on this day that comes only once
every four years?

4년에 한 번 있는 오늘, 뭘 하면서 보냈어?

20

20

20

20

20

Disney
ZOOTOPIA
2
3
March

1

**Do you remember how many times
you laughed out loud today?**

오늘 하루 크게 소리 내어 몇 번 웃었는지 기억해?

20

20

20

20

20

How many times did you look at the sky today?

오늘 하루 하늘을 몇 번 올려다보았어?

20

20

20

20

20

3

How do you respond when someone misunderstands you?

누군가 나를 오해했을 때, 너는 어떻게 반응해?

20

20

20

20

20

Tell me your favorite lyrics.

좋아하는 노래 중 가장 좋아하는 가사를 알려줘.

20

20

20

20

20

5

What part of yourself do you hope will never change,
even decades from now?

10년, 20년, 30년이 지나도 변하지 않았으면 하는
네 모습에는 뭐가 있니?

20

20

20

20

20

What challenge do I want to take on today?

오늘 네가 도전하고 싶은 일은 뭐야?

20

20

20

20

20

1

Do you think you're a perfectionist?

스스로 완벽주의자라고 생각해?

20

20

20

20

20

What do you think you're lacking?
너에게 부족한 것은 무엇이라고 생각해?

20

20

20

20

20

9

When was the last time you were angry? What's the story?

최근에 가장 화가 났던 때는 언제야? 무슨 일로 그랬어?

20

20

20

20

20

Let's share the moments we were grateful for today,
even the little ones.

사소해도 좋아, 오늘 하루 감사했던 일을 찾아보자.

20

20

20

20

20

11

What was the happiest time of your life?

살아오면서 가장 행복했던 시간은?

20

20

20

20

20

What small act of courage did I show today?

오늘 네가 용기 낸 작은 행동은 뭐였어?

20

20

20

20

20

13

What do you do first when you wake up in the morning?

아침에 일어나서 가장 먼저 하는 일은?

20

20

20

20

20

14

When did you feel a sense of achievement in recent years?

최근에 성취감을 느낀 것은 어떤 때였어?

20

20

20

20

20

15

What has been the most difficult time in your life so far?

지금까지의 인생에서 가장 힘들었던 시간은?

20

20

20

20

20

16

What do you want to hear the most today?

오늘 네가 가장 듣고 싶은 말은?

20

20

20

20

20

17

Do you ever feel lonely? When?

외롭다고 느낄 때가 있어? 언제 그렇니?

20

20

20

20

20

What is the most delicious dish you can make?

네가 가장 자신 있게 만들 수 있는 요리는?

20

20

20

20

20

19

What did you have for breakfast, lunch, and dinner today?

오늘의 아침, 점심, 저녁 메뉴는?

20

20

20

20

20

Do you have a secret you've never told anyone?

아무에게도 말하지 않은 비밀 한 가지는?

20

20

20

20

20

21

Describe your current hairstyle as romantically as possible.

지금 네 헤어스타일을 가능한 한 낭만적으로 묘사해줘.

20

20

20

20

20

What is your favorite accessory? How often do you wear it?

가장 좋아하는 액세서리는 어떤 거야? 얼마나 자주 착용해?

20

20

20

20

20

23

What do you think you can do to achieve your goal?

목표를 이루기 위해 무슨 일까지 할 수 있을 것 같아?

20

20

20

20

20

Are you a morning person or a night person?

너는 아침형 인간일까, 저녁형 인간일까?

20

20

20

20

20

25

What was the most demanding thing you've done this week?

이번 주에 가장 무리했던 일은 뭐였어?

20

20

20

20

20

If you were to buy a car, what kind would you want?

차를 산다면 어떤 차를 타고 싶어?

20

20

20

20

20

27

Is there anyone you feel you'll never be able to reconcile with?
Why do you think you can't make up with them?

평생 화해할 수 없을 것 같은 사람이 있어?
왜 화해할 수 없을 것 같아?

20

20

20

20

20

What is the most important value to you in relationships?

네가 사람을 만날 때 가장 중요하게 생각하는 가치는 뭐야?

20

20

20

20

20

29

If you were to say something warm to your best friend,
what would it be?

친한 친구에게 따뜻한 말을 건넨다면, 무슨 말을 하고 싶어?

20

20

20

20

20

What is the most regrettable thing you've done for love?

사랑 때문에 저질렀던 가장 후회되는 일은?

20

20

20

20

20

31

Do you like to talk? or to listen?

평소 이야기 하는 것을 좋아해? 아니면 듣는 것을 좋아해?

20

20

20

20

20

zootopia 2
4
April

1

What do you think when you see the cherry blossoms this year?

올해 벚꽃을 보면 어떤 생각이 들어?

20

20

20

20

20

Is there a travel destination you want to go to alone?

혼자 떠나고 싶은 여행지가 있어?

20

20

20

20

20

3

What do you remember from today?

오늘 있었던 일 중 무엇이 기억에 남아?

20

20

20

20

20

4

What do you want to say to yourself now?

지금 스스로에게 해주고 싶은 말은?

20

20

20

20

20

5

Who was the first person you met today?

오늘 가장 먼저 만난 사람은 누구야?

20

20

20

20

20

Who do you want to go with if you go on a trip?

여행을 떠난다면 누구랑 같이 가고 싶어?

20

20

20

20

20

7

If you could make a law, what kind of law would you like to make?

네가 법을 만들 수 있다면 어떤 법을 만들고 싶어?

20

20

20

20

20

8

Could you give up everything else to gain something?
If so, what would it be?

어떤 것을 얻기 위해 다른 모든 것을 포기할 수 있을까?
그렇다면 그건 무엇일까?

20

20

20

20

20

9

Do you have a motto?

좌우명이 있어?

20

20

20

20

20

10

Was there anything you couldn't have no matter how hard you tried?

노력해도 가질 수 없었던 것이 있었어?

20

20

20

20

20

11

What do you want to try the most this year?

올해 가장 도전해보고 싶은 것은 뭐야?

20

20

20

20

20

12

What is the most memorable passage you've read recently?

최근에 읽은 책 중 기억나는 구절은?

20

20

20

20

20

13

What can't you endure?

네가 도저히 참을 수 없는 것은?

20

20

20

20

20

14

Is there something you want to fix?

고치고 싶은 부분이 있어?

20

20

20

20

20

15

What did you drink most often over the past month?

한 달 동안 가장 자주 마신 음료는 뭐였어?

20

20

20

20

20

16

Can you describe your favorite scent in more than two sentences?

가장 좋아하는 향기를 두 문장 이상으로 설명한다면?

20

20

20

20

20

17

What are you truly hoping for right now?

지금 너는 무엇을 진심으로 바라고 있어?

20

20

20

20

20

18

If there's someone you're most sorry about right now, who is it?

지금 가장 미안하게 생각되는 사람이 있다면 누구야?

APR

20

20

20

20

20

19

What's the last movie you watched?

가장 최근에 본 영화는 뭐야?

20

20

20

20

20

20

What's the keyword you search most these days?

요즘 가장 많이 검색하는 키워드는 뭐야?

20

20

20

20

20

21

Is there anyone you really want to meet
at the last moment of your life?

삶의 마지막 순간에 꼭 부르고 싶은, 만나고 싶은 사람이 있어?

20

20

20

20

20

22

Who did you have your best meal with?

가장 근사했던 식사는 어디서 누구와 함께한 자리였어?

20

20

20

20

20

23

In what ways are you trying to heal me?

어떤 방식으로 나를 치유하려고 노력해?

20

20

20

20

20

Is there anyone you want to get closer to?

더 가까워지고 싶은 사람이 있어?

20

20

20

20

20

25

Name something you haven't used since you bought it.

구입한 뒤 한 번도 안 쓴 물건은 어떤 거야?

20

20

20

20

20

Is there anything you cannot forgive?

이것만큼은 용서할 수 없다고 생각하는 게 있어?

20

20

20

20

20

27

What kind of flowers do you like?

요즘은 어떤 꽃을 좋아해?

20

20

20

20

20

Do you have anyone or situation that you're nervous about?

네가 긴장하는 상대나 상황이 있어?

20

20

20

20

20

29

How do you find support and comfort
in your relationships with friends?

친구와의 관계에서 어떤 지지와 위로를 받고 있어?

20

20

20

20

20

Who's the first person you think of when you eat delicious food?

맛있는 음식을 먹을 때 가장 먼저 생각나는 사람은 누구야?

20

20

20

20

20

Zootopia 2
5
May

1

What was the most recent call you received about?

가장 최근에 받은 전화는 무슨 소식이야?

20

20

20

20

20

2

What time did you get up this morning? Why was it that time?

오늘 아침에 몇 시에 일어났어? 왜 그때 일어난 거야?

20

20

20

20

20

3

How many things can you do at once?

한 번에 몇 개의 일을 처리할 수 있어?

20

20

20

20

20

What was the most interesting thing that happened
on the trip?

여행지에서 생겼던 가장 재미있었던 일은 뭐였어?

20

20

20

20

20

5

What was the gift you most wanted to receive
in your childhood?

어렸을 때 가장 받고 싶었던 선물은 뭐였어?

20

20

20

20

20

Why do you think your existence is so special?

네 존재가 특별한 이유는 뭐라고 생각해?

20

20

20

20

20

7

What is the most memorable gift you've ever received?

가장 기억에 남는 선물은 뭐였어?

20

20

20

20

20

When was the last time you had a meal with your parents?

가장 최근에 부모님과 식사한 때는 언제야?

20

20

20

20

20

MAY

9

Do you have any musical instruments you can play?
If not, what instrument would you like to learn?

연주할 수 있는 악기가 있어? 혹시 없다면 어떤 악기를 배우고 싶어?

20

20

20

20

20

What's the oldest present you have and who gave it to you?

가지고 있는 것 중에 가장 오래된 선물은 뭐야?
그리고 누가 준 거야?

20

20

20

20

20

11

Have you had a moment recently that felt warm to you?

최근에 따뜻함이라고 느껴졌던 순간이 있어?

20

20

20

20

20

Describe the clothes you're wearing today?

오늘 입은 옷을 설명해줄래?

20

20

20

20

20

13

When did you go to bed yesterday?

어제 몇 시에 잠자리에 들었어?

20

20

20

20

20

Write down the title of the most important news you read today.

오늘 읽은 뉴스 중 가장 중요했던 뉴스 제목을 적어봐.

20

20

20

20

20

15

Is there anything you really want to say to your parents?

부모님께 꼭 하고 싶은 말이 있다면?

20

20

20

20

20

16

Has anyone ever made something for you?

누군가가 너를 위해 무언가를 직접 만들어준 적이 있어?

20

20

20

20

20

17

What is your favorite sport?

네가 가장 좋아하는 운동은 뭐야?

20

20

20

20

20

What kind of animal do you like as a pet?

반려동물을 기른다면 어떤 동물이 좋아?

20

20

20

20

20

19

What food comes to mind when you're sick?

아플 때 생각나는 음식은 뭐야?

20

20

20

20

20

Among the people around you, who turned out to be the most different from your first impression?

주변 사람들 중 첫인상과 가장 다른 사람은 누구야?

20

20

20

20

20

21

**When was the last time you exercised until
you were out of breath?**

마지막으로 숨이 꽉 찰 정도까지 운동했던 건 언제야?

20

20

20

20

20

22

What's the firmest rejection you've made lately?

최근에 가장 단호하게 거절했던 일은 뭐야?

20

20

20

20

20

23

What is the most precious item you own?

갖고 있는 물건 중에 가장 아끼는 물건은 뭐야?

20

20

20

20

20

24

What's the biggest mistake you've made lately?

최근에 한 가장 큰 실수는?

20

20

20

20

20

25

What was the most hasty decision you've ever made,
and what was the result?

가장 성급한 결정을 내렸던 일과 그 결과를 알려줄래?

20

20

20

20

20

Can you find something good for someone
who isn't favorable to you?

네게 호의적이지 않은 사람에게도 좋은 점을 찾을 수 있을까?

20

20

20

20

20

27

What would be your dream job?

네가 생각하는 꿈의 직장은 어디야?

20

20

20

20

20

What is your favorite cartoon?

가장 좋아하는 만화는 뭐야?

20

20

20

20

20

29

What is your favorite way to spend the weekend?

주말을 보내는 너만의 가장 행복한 방법은?

20

20

20

20

20

Is there any new field that you've been interested in lately?

최근 새롭게 흥미를 느끼게 된 분야가 있어?

20

20

20

20

20

31

What's the most pleasant word you've heard recently?
최근에 들었던 말 중 가장 기분 좋은 말은?

20

20

20

20

20

Disney
ZOOTOPIA
2
6
June
POLICE
BOGO

1

What is the one thing that made you happy today?

오늘 하루를 기쁘게 만든 한 가지는 뭐야?

20

20

20

20

20

What goal do you most want to achieve?

가장 이루고 싶은 목표는 뭐야?

20

20

20

20

20

Is there anyone who makes you feel awkward or
uncomfortable at home or at work?

가족이나 직장에 어색하고 불편한 사람이 있어?
왜 그 사람이 불편할까?

20

20

20

20

20

4

Can you write down the first sentence of page 105
of the nearest book?

가장 가까이에 있는 책의 105쪽 첫 문장이 뭔지 적어줄래?

20

20

20

20

20

What app do you use the most these days?
How often do you use it in a week?

요즘 가장 자주 사용하는 앱(App)은 어떤 거야?
일주일에 얼마나 사용해?

20

20

20

20

20

Tell me your 3 favorite words!
가장 사랑하는 단어 3가지를 알려줘!

20

20

20

20

20

7

How many times have you stayed up all night in the past six months? Why did you have to stay up?

반년 동안 밤을 새운 적이 몇 번이나 있어? 왜 밤을 새워야 했어?

20

20

20

20

20

What was the content of the mail or text message that required the biggest courage before sending?

보내기 전에 가장 큰 용기가 필요했던 메일이나 문자는
어떤 내용이었어?

20

20

20

20

20

9

Have you ever thought that you shouldn't be like this?

이대로면 안 된다는 생각이 들었던 적이 있어?

20

20

20

20

20

Who's your favorite artist?

좋아하는 예술가는 누구야?

20

20

20

20

20

JUN

11

What was the most embarrassing thing
that happened this year?

올해 있었던 가장 당황스러운 일은 뭐였어?

20

20

20

20

20

12

Do you have a place that comes to mind when it rains?

비가 내리면 떠오르는 장소가 있어?

20

20

20

20

20

13

What is your MBTI?

너의 MBTI는 뭐야?

20

20

20

20

20

14

What was it that you didn't regret after you threw it away?

버리고 나서도 후회하지 않았던 것은 뭐였어?

20

20

20

20

20

15

Can you describe the color of the ocean that comes to
your mind right now?

지금 떠오르는 바다의 색깔을 묘사해줄래?

20

20

20

20

20

16

What movie have you watched more than twice, and why?

두 번 이상 본 영화는 어떤 거야? 이유는 뭐였어?

20

20

20

20

20

17

Where do you usually get information when you have a question?

궁금한 게 생겼을 때 주로 어디서 정보를 얻어?

20

20

20

20

20

What is your favorite food?

네가 가장 좋아하는 음식은 뭐야?

20

20

20

20

20

19

What word would best describe you?

너와 가장 잘 어울리는 단어를 하나 골라본다면?

20

20

20

20

20

If you could give yourself a nickname, what would it be?

네 별명을 스스로 붙여본다면?

20

20

20

20

20

21

I wonder how often you spend your time alone.

혼자만의 시간을 얼마나 자주 갖는지 궁금해.

20

20

20

20

20

If you could be someone else for just one day, who would you be?

단 하루만 다른 사람이 될 수 있다면 누가 되고 싶어?

20

20

20

20

20

23

What makes you go to see a doctor recently?

가장 최근에 병원에 갔던 이유는 뭐였어?

20

20

20

20

20

24

Do you have any medicine or nutritional supplements?

챙겨 먹는 약이나 영양제가 있어?

20

20

20

20

20

25

How long can you wait for someone else?

얼마나 오랫동안 다른 사람을 기다릴 수 있니?

20

20

20

20

20

Among your friends, who lives the furthest?

가장 멀리 사는 친구는 누구야?

20

20

20

20

20

Let's write a positive message to your future self!

미래의 나에게 전하고 싶은 긍정 메시지를 적어보자!

20

20

20

20

20

28

Where was your destination on your last trip,
and what transportation did you use?

가장 최근에 떠난 여행지는 어디였어?
어떤 교통수단을 이용했니?

20

20

20

20

20

29

The mountains or the sea? The countryside or the city?
Where would you prefer to travel?

산 VS 바다, 시골 VS 도시. 여행을 떠난다면 어디가 좋아?

20

20

20

20

20

If you could love only one person for your entire life,
who would it be?

평생 한 사람만 사랑한다면 누구일 것 같아?

20

20

20

20

20

Zootopia 2
7
July

1

What was the most useless gift you've ever received?

여태껏 받았던 것 중 가장 쓸모없었던 선물은 뭐였어?

20

20

20

20

20

What was your warmest memory of childhood?

어린 시절을 떠올릴 때 가장 포근했던 기억은 뭐야?

20

20

20

20

20

3

What is something you experienced for the first time recently?

최근에 처음으로 경험한 일은 뭐야?

20

20

20

20

20

4

What is something you should have given up earlier in your life?

지금까지의 인생에서 포기했어야 했던 것은 뭐였어?

20

20

20

20

20

What does abundance in your life mean?

네가 원하는 풍요로움은 어떤 거야?

20

20

20

20

20

If you were a season, what would you be?

네가 계절이 된다면 어떤 계절이 되고 싶어?

20

20

20

20

20

JUL

7

What was the most pleasant thought you had today?
오늘, 가장 기분 좋은 상상은 뭐였어?

20

20

20

20

20

What do you do to boost your self-esteem?

자존감을 높이기 위해 어떤 노력을 해?

20

20

20

20

20

9

If you could change your name, what would you change it to?

이름을 바꾼다면 어떤 이름으로 바꾸고 싶어?

20

20

20

20

20

10

What kind of adversity do you think you should overcome?

헤쳐나가야 할 네 몫의 역경이 있니?

20

20

20

20

20

11

What do you do when you feel an irresistible temptation?

참기 힘든 유혹을 느낄 땐 어떻게 해?

20

20

20

20

20

If you could be a star, what kind of star would you be?

별이 될 수 있다면 어떤 별이 되고 싶어?

20

20

20

20

20

13

What book title have you seen the most in your life?

여러 번 본 책 제목은 뭐야?

20

20

20

20

20

14

How do you feel when you think of tomorrow?

내일을 생각하면 어떤 기분이 들어?

20

20

20

20

20

15

What's the best thing about being your age right now?

지금 너의 나이가 되어서 좋은 점은 뭐가 있을까?

20

20

20

20

20

16

Have you ever forgiven someone?

누군가를 용서해 본 적이 있어?

20

20

20

20

20

17

Do you have a small wish of your own?

너만이 가진 작은 소망이 있다면 알려줄래?

20

20

20

20

20

What did you have for dinner tonight?

오늘 저녁은 뭘 먹었어?

20

20

20

20

20

19

Do you have your own walking route?

너만의 산책 코스가 있어?

20

20

20

20

20

Do you have your own methods for improving your memory?

기억을 잘하기 위한 너만의 비법이 있어?

20

20

20

20

20

21

Is there a gift you'd like to give yourself?

너 스스로에게 주고 싶은 선물이 있어?

20

20

20

20

20

What's the last thing on your check list before you go on a trip?

여행을 떠나기 전에 가장 마지막으로 체크하는 건 뭐야?

22

20

20

20

20

20

23

Did you learn anything new today?

오늘 새롭게 배운 게 있어?

20

20

20

20

20

When was the last time you danced?

가장 마지막으로 춤춘 건 언제였어?

24

20

20

20

20

20

25

Express your emotions for today in colors!

오늘의 감정을 색으로 표현해줘!

20

20

20

20

20

What type of person do you like?

너는 어떤 타입의 사람을 좋아해?

20

20

20

20

20

27

Have you ever traveled alone?

혼자서 여행을 가본 적이 있어?

20

20

20

20

20

Do you think marriage is an important factor in happiness,
or do you think there are other important factors?

결혼이 행복에 중요한 요소라고 생각해?
아니면 다른 중요한 요소들이 더 있다고 생각해?

20

20

20

20

20

29

Is there someone you respect?

존경하는 사람이 있어?

20

20

20

20

20

30

Do you have any mystery you'd like to solve?

해결하고 싶은 '미스터리'가 있어?

20

20

20

20

20

Is there any period of your life you wish you could erase?

인생에서 가장 지우고 싶은 때가 있니?

20

20

20

20

20

Disney
ZOOTOPIA 2
8
August

1

What kind of partner would you like to work with?

네가 함께 일하고 싶은 파트너는 어떤 유형이야?

20

20

20

20

20

What is your top priority when you have to make a choice?

무언가를 선택할 때 가장 우선적으로 생각하는 것은 뭐야?

20

20

20

20

20

3

Is what you're doing now what you've always wanted to do?

네가 지금 하고 있는 일이 가장 하고 싶은 일이야?

20

20

20

20

20

4

Tell me your favorite word and what it means.

네가 좋아하는 단어와 그 의미를 말해줘.

20

20

20

20

20

5

If you were to say "I love you" to someone today,
who would it be?

오늘 누군가에게 "사랑해"라고 말한다면, 누구에게 하고 싶어?

20

20

20

20

20

6

Who do you think understands you best?

너를 가장 잘 이해해주는 사람은 누구라고 생각해?

20

20

20

20

20

7

What do you do when you feel overwhelmed or stuck?

마음이 답답할 때 어떻게 해?

20

20

20

20

20

Just tell me three of your strengths.

네가 생각하는 너의 장점을 세 가지만 이야기해줘.

20

20

20

20

20

9

Just tell me three of your weaknesses.

네가 생각하는 너의 단점을 세 가지만 이야기해줘.

20

20

20

20

20

What were you thinking about last night before you fell asleep?

지난 밤, 잠들기 전에 어떤 생각을 했어?

20

20

20

20

20

11

Is there something you really want to protect?

꼭 지키고 싶은 무언가가 있어?

20

20

20

20

20

What do you regret not doing when you were a teenager?

10대에 해보지 않아서 후회되는 일은 뭐가 있을까?

20

20

20

20

20

15

Do you have a favorite painting?

좋아하는 그림이 있어?

20

20

20

20

20

16

Where do you find yourself going often these days?

요즘 정말 자주 가는 공간은 어디야?

20

20

20

20

20

17

How many friends do you open up to?

속마음을 털어놓는 친구가 몇 명 있어?

20

20

20

20

20

18

What do you want to say to yourself at the age of 20?

스무 살의 너에게 하고 싶은 말은?

20

20

20

20

20

19

What's in your bag now?

지금 네 가방 속에 들어 있는 것들은?

20

20

20

20

20

Have you had a moment recently when you felt truly
connected to someone?

최근에 누군가에게 진심이 느껴지는 순간이 있었어?

20

20

20

20

20

21

Which character from a book or movie do you admire the most?

네가 책이나 영화 속 캐릭터 중 가장 동경하는 사람은
어떤 사람이야?

20

20

20

20

20

What is the thing you most regret doing to someone you love?

사랑하는 사람에게 했던 가장 후회스러운 행동은 뭐야?

20

20

20

20

20

23

Do you have a habit that comes out when you're nervous?

긴장할 때 튀어나오는 버릇이 있어?

20

20

20

20

20

To whom did you last write a handwritten letter?

마지막으로 쓴 손편지의 상대는 누구야?

20

20

20

20

20

25

If you could have a superpower, what would it be?

만약 초능력을 가지게 된다면 어떤 능력을 가지고 싶어?

20

20

20

20

20

Has anyone been kind to you today?

오늘 너에게 친절히 대해준 사람이 있어?

20

20

20

20

20

27

What was the funniest game or activity you enjoyed
in your childhood?

어린 시절 가장 재미있게 했던 놀이는?

20

20

20

20

20

What was the happiest thing in the day?

오늘 하루 가장 행복했던 일은?

20

20

20

20

20

Do you have a habit that you can't fix?

고치고 싶은데 못 고치고 있는 습관이 있어?

AUG

20

20

20

20

20

What moment gave me the greatest courage today?

오늘 나에게 가장 큰 용기를 준 순간은 언제였어?

20

20

20

20

20

When do you feel happy in your life right now?

지금 삶에서 행복하다고 느끼는 순간은 언제야?

20

20

20

20

20

Disney
ZOOTOPIA 2
9
September
DR. FUZZBY

1

Where do you think you will be living when you are sixty

예순 살이 되었을 때 너는 어디에서 살고 있을까?

20

20

20

20

20

2

What do you want to cut off the most from your life?

네 삶에서 가장 끊어내고 싶은 것이 있다면?

20

20

20

20

20

3

Who was the first person you bought a gift for this year?

올해 처음 산 선물은 누구를 위한 거였어?

20

20

20

20

20

What is the most memorable dream you've had recently?

최근 꾼 꿈 중에서 가장 기억에 남는 내용은 뭐야?

20

20

20

20

20

5

What do you think happiness is?

행복이란 뭐라고 생각해?

20

20

20

20

20

If you could go back 30 minutes, when would you go back?

과거로 30분만 돌아갈 수 있다면 언제로 돌아갈 거야?

20

20

20

20

20

7

Do you think love can change people, and in what ways?

사랑이 사람을 변화시킬 수 있다고 생각해?
어떤 방식으로 변화가 일어날 수 있을까?

20

20

20

20

20

Are you a neat person or a messy person?

깔끔한 편이야, 지저분한 편이야?

8

20

20

20

20

20

9

Who made you laugh today?

오늘 너를 웃게 한 존재는 누구야?

20

20

20

20

20

10

Express yourself in color today.

오늘의 나를 색으로 표현해보자.

20

20

20

20

20

11

When was the last time you looked up at the night sky?

마지막으로 밤하늘을 올려다 본 게 언제야?

20

20

20

20

20

12

What is your least favorite housework and your favorite housework?

가장 하기 싫은 집안일과 가장 좋아하는 집안일이 뭐야?

20

20

20

20

20

13

How are you feeling these days?

요즘 너의 컨디션은 어때?

20

20

20

20

20

14

What's the condition of your room or house right now?

지금 네 방이나 집의 상태는 어때?

20

20

20

20

20

15

Do you know what your health is like now?

자신의 건강이 지금 어떤 상태인지 알고 있어?

20

20

20

20

20

16

When was the last time you cried?

마지막으로 울었던 때는 언제였어?

20

20

20

20

20

17

What would you like to say to your future self?

미래의 나에게 어떤 말을 해주고 싶어?

20

20

20

20

20

18

Where do you spend most of your time during the day?

하루 중 가장 오래 시간을 보내는 곳은 어디야?

20

20

20

20

20

19

Can you describe your life by one word?

오늘까지의 네 삶을 한 마디로 정리해보면 어때?

20

20

20

20

20

Who's the closest person in your family?

가족 중 가장 가까운 사람은 누구야?

20

20

20

20

20

21

What are you waiting for that makes you happy?

어떤 걸 기다리는 시간이 제일 행복해?

20

20

20

20

20

How do you feel when you visit a new place?

새로운 장소를 방문하면 어떤 느낌이 들어?

20

20

20

20

20

23

What is your own healing routine?

나만의 힐링 루틴을 찾아볼까?

20

20

20

20

20

Which do you prefer, light or dark?

빛과 어둠 중 어떤 쪽을 선호해?

20

20

20

20

20

25

Write down one bias I have—what can I do to let it go?

내가 가진 편견 하나를 적어보고,
그것을 내려놓기 위해 무엇을 할 수 있을까?

20

20

20

20

20

What's your special ability?

네가 가장 잘하는 건 뭐야?

20

20

20

20

20

27

Do the people you find attractive have anything in common?

네가 매력적이라고 생각하는 사람들에게 공통점이 있다면?

20

20

20

20

20

Do the people you don't want to get close to
have anything in common?

네가 가까워지고 싶지 않은 사람들에게 공통점이 있다면?

20

20

20

20

20

29

Who was your first love?

첫사랑은 어떤 사람이었어?

20

20

20

20

20

Which café do you often go to, and why?

자주 가는 카페와, 그곳을 자주 찾는 이유는?

20

20

20

20

20

Zootopia 2
10
October

1

What would you do first if you were lost in a strange place?

낯선 곳에서 길을 잃었다면 가장 먼저 뭘 할 것 같아?

20

20

20

20

20

Are there any things you always need to take with you
when you go out?

외출할 때 꼭 챙겨야 하는 것들이 있어?

20

20

20

20

20

3

Who seems the happiest around you?

주변에서 가장 행복해 보이는 사람은 누구야?

20

20

20

20

20

Describe today's autumn weather.

오늘의 가을을 묘사해줘.

20

20

20

20

20

5

What's your favorite TV show right now?

현재 가장 좋아하는 TV프로그램은 뭐야?

20

20

20

20

20

6

Have you ever had an experience where your
imagination came true?

상상이 현실이 된 경험을 한 적 있어?

20

20

20

20

20

7

Can you give the place you're in right now a creative new name?

지금 네가 있는 장소의 이름을 상상력이 들어간 이름으로
고쳐본다면?

20

20

20

20

20

What does it mean to love me?

나를 사랑한다는 것은 무엇일까?

20

20

20

20

20

9

Can you truly tell yourself "Good night" today?

오늘은 진심으로 'Good Night'이라고 말할 수 있어?

20

20

20

20

20

10

How do you deal with difficult situations when they come up?

힘든 일을 맞닥뜨렸을 때 어떤 마음으로 처리해?

20

20

20

20

20

If you love someone now, what do you like most about him/her?

지금 사랑하는 사람이 있다면 그 사람의 어떤 점이 가장 좋아?

20

20

20

20

20

Do you have a favorite animal?

좋아하는 동물이 있어?

20

20

20

20

20

13

Do you have any favorite characters from animations,
movies, dramas, or novels?

애니메이션, 영화, 드라마, 소설 속 좋아하는 캐릭터가 있어?

20

20

20

20

20

What does the word "success" mean to you?

너에게 '성공'이란 어떤 거야?

20

20

20

20

20

Are there any celebrities you are interested in right now?

지금 관심 있는 연예인이 있어?

20

20

20

20

20

What do you do when you've done all the work you have to do?

해야 할 일을 다 하고 나면 어떻게 해?

20

20

20

20

20

17

How much do you plan your trips before you leave?

여행가기 전에 계획을 어디까지 세워?

20

20

20

20

20

Who is your best friend?

가장 친한 친구는 누구야?

20

20

20

20

20

19

Do you tend to follow your heart when making
important decisions?

중요한 결정을 내릴 때 마음이 시키는 대로 따르는 편이야?

20

20

20

20

20

20

How do you respond when your friends or family are sad?

친구나 가족이 슬퍼할 때 어떻게 위로해줘?

20

20

20

20

20

21

What idea or plan just came to your mind?

지금 머릿속에 떠오른 아이디어나 계획은 어떤 거야?

20

20

20

20

20

22

If I were to compare you to an animal, which one would you be?

너를 동물에 비유하자면 어떤 동물에 가까울까?

20

20

20

20

20

23

How many times did you hear your name today?

오늘 너의 이름을 몇 번 들어봤어?

20

20

20

20

20

24

What's the biggest problem you have right now?

지금 가지고 있는 가장 큰 고민은 뭐야?

20

20

20

20

20

25

What's the biggest change that has happened to you
in the past year?

지난 한 해 동안 너에게 있었던 가장 큰 변화는 뭐야?

20

20

20

20

20

Have you ever liked something at first sight? What was it?

첫눈에 반했던 사물이 있어? 어떤 거였어?

20

20

20

20

20

27

Have you ever had an experience that made you see someone
in a new light, and how did it affect your relationship?

누군가를 새로운 시각으로 보게 된 경험이 있어?
그 경험이 관계에 어떤 영향을 미쳤어?

20

20

20

20

20

28

Who has supported you, and how has their support changed you

너를 응원해 준 사람은 누구이며, 그 덕분에 무엇이 달라졌어?

20

20

20

20

20

29

If you were to describe yourself in three words these days,
what would they be?

요즘의 나를 세 단어로 표현해 본다면?

20

20

20

20

20

30

What has made you feel the most uneasy lately?
What's going on with it?

최근에 가장 불안했던 일이 뭐야? 그 일은 지금 어떻게 되었어?

20

20

20

20

20

31

Is there anything you always carry around with you?

항상 몸에 지니고 다니는 물건이 있어?

20

20

20

20

20

zootopia 2
11
November

1

What are three things you must have in your own space?

너만의 공간에 꼭 놓아두는 세 가지는 뭐야?

20

20

20

20

20

2

What are three things you would take to a deserted island?

무인도에 꼭 가져가야 할 세 가지는 뭘까?

20

20

20

20

20

Where was the last place you saw the sunrise?

마지막으로 일출을 본 곳은 어디였어?

20

20

20

20

20

4

Who have you been meeting the most these days,
and what do you usually do together?

요즘 누구와 가장 많이 만나고 있어? 만나서 뭐 해?

20

20

20

20

20

5

What kind of person do you think is a truly good or 'right' person?

올바른 사람은 어떤 사람이라고 생각해?

20

20

20

20

20

Do you think you can tell the exact moment you fall in love?

사랑에 빠지는 순간을 정확히 알 수 있을까?

20

20

20

20

20

7

What kind of weather do you like?

어떤 날씨를 좋아해?

20

20

20

20

20

If you want to see someone right now, tell me their name
and how you feel about them.

지금 누군가를 보고 싶다면, 그 사람의 이름과 느낌을 말해줘.

20

20

20

20

20

9

What kind of parent do you want to be?

어떤 부모가 되고 싶어?

20

20

20

20

20

10

How do you change when you love someone?

너는 누군가를 사랑할 때, 어떻게 변해?

20

20

20

20

20

11

What words of comfort do you need right now?

지금, 너에게 필요한 위로의 말은 뭐야?

20

20

20

20

20

12

Are you satisfied with your life now? If not, why?

지금 너의 생활에 충분히 만족해? 그렇지 않다면 이유는?

20

20

20

20

20

13

If you could look into your future, what age would you want to see?

너의 미래를 미리 볼 수 있다면
몇 살 때의 너를 확인해 보고 싶어?

20

20

20

20

20

Who makes you laugh the most these days?

요즘 너를 가장 많이 웃게 하는 사람은 누구야?

14

20

20

20

20

20

NOV

15

What would you like to do on a snowy day?

눈이 올 때 하고 싶은 건 뭐야?

20

20

20

20

20

When you're going through a hard time, what gives you hope?

힘든 시기를 보낼 때, 희망이 되는 것은 뭐라고 생각해?

20

20

20

20

20

NOV

17

Is there a place where you go to cry alone?

혼자 울고 싶을 때 찾는 장소가 있어?

20

20

20

20

20

What would you like to do first if you won the lottery?

복권에 당첨된다면 가장 먼저 무엇을 하고 싶어?

20

20

20

20

20

19

When do you think the turning point of your life was?

인생의 전환점이었다고 생각하는 때는 언제야?

20

20

20

20

20

Is there something you don't want to hear from someone else?

다른 사람에게 듣고 싶지 않은 말이 있다면?

20

20

20

20

20

21

What do you usually do when you're alone?

혼자 있을 때 주로 뭘 해?

20

20

20

20

20

22

Let me know if you've learned any important lessons from your reading!

독서를 통해 배운 중요한 교훈이 있으면 알려줘!

20

20

20

20

20

23

What title would you choose if you wrote your autobiography?

너의 인생을 책으로 쓴다면 제목은 무엇이 될까?

20

20

20

20

20

Is there anything that makes your heart race these days?

요즘 너의 가슴을 뛰게 하는 일이 있어?

20

20

20

20

20

What's the most recent incident that embarrassed you?

최근에 가장 너를 당황하게 만든 사건은 뭐야?

20

20

20

20

20

What do you think love is?

나에게 사랑은 뭐라고 생각해?

20

20

20

20

20

NOV

27

How would you rate your life satisfaction out of five stars?

현재 삶의 만족도는 별 다섯 개 중 몇 개야?

20

20

20

20

20

What's a song you can't miss on your playlist?

플레이리스트에서 빠지지 않는 노래는 뭐야?

20

20

20

20

20

29

Which do you prefer, summer or winter?

여름이 좋아, 겨울이 좋아?

20

20

20

20

20

What do you want to do when the first snow comes?

첫눈이 오면 하고 싶은 일은?

20

20

20

20

20

Disney
ZOOTOPIA
2
12
December

1

Where do you want to go when the first snow comes?

첫눈이 올 때 어디에 가고 싶어?

20

20

20

20

20

2

If you were born again, what would you like to be?

다시 태어난다면 무엇으로 태어나고 싶어?

20

20

20

20

20

What would you like to do if you had free time for a day?

하루 동안 자유시간이 주어지면 뭘 하고 싶어?

20

20

20

20

20

4

What is your favorite word these days?

요즘 가장 좋아하는 단어는 뭐야?

20

20

20

20

20

5

What is the most memorable conversation you had with your parents today?

오늘 부모님과 한 대화 중 기억에 남는 것은 뭐야?

20

20

20

20

20

How do you feel when you think of your first love?

첫사랑을 생각하면 어떤 감정이 떠올라?

20

20

20

20

20

7

What do you want to say to someone who hates you?

너를 미워하는 사람에게 어떤 말을 해주고 싶어?

20

20

20

20

20

8

Have you been deeply moved by anything lately?

최근에 크게 감동을 받은 적이 있어?

20

20

20

20

20

9

What would you do if today were the last day of your life?

오늘이 인생 마지막 날이라면 무엇을 하고 싶어?

20

20

20

20

20

How would you write the first sentence of your autobiography?

자서전을 쓴다면 첫 문장을 어떻게 쓰고 싶어?

20

20

20

20

20

11

Is there an area where you feel you've grown this year?

올해 내가 성장했다고 느껴지는 부분이 있어?

20

20

20

20

20

This year, did you accomplish the goals you set, or not?

올해 초 계획한 것들 중에서 이룬 것과 이루지 못한 것은 뭐야?

20

20

20

20

20

13

Have you ever approached a complete stranger and
started a conversation?

처음 보는 사람에게 무작정 다가가서 말을 걸어본 적이 있어?

20

20

20

20

20

14

What achievement made me most proud this year?
올해 나를 가장 자랑스럽게 만든 일은 뭐였어?

20

20

20

20

20

15

Can you tell me about your favorite outfit?

네가 가장 좋아하는 옷에 대해 설명해줄래?

20

20

20

20

20

Have you ever been on a blind date? How did it go?

소개팅을 해본 적이 있어? 결과는 어땠어?

20

20

20

20

20

17

Which animal would you like to have, a dog or a cat?

강아지와 고양이 중에 기르고 싶은 동물은?

20

20

20

20

20

Let's write a resolution that will help you spend
next year meaningfully!

내년을 보람차게 보낼 수 있는 다짐을 써보자!

20

20

20

20

20

19

Do you have any questions you would like to ask?

사람들한테 즐겨하는 질문이 있어?

20

20

20

20

20

Who is someone you want to treat with more warmth
going forward?

앞으로 더 따뜻하게 대하고 싶은 사람이 누구야?

20

20

20

20

20

What is your favorite day of the year?

1년 중에 가장 좋아하는 날은?

20

20

20

20

20

Do you know the bestselling book of the year?

올해의 베스트셀러를 알고 있어?

20

20

20

20

20

DEC

How would you summarize the meaning of
"love" in one sentence?

사랑'의 의미를 한 문장으로 요약한다면?

20

20

20

20

20

What gift do you most want to receive for Christmas?

크리스마스에 받고 싶은 선물은 뭐야?

20

20

20

20

20

Merry Christmas! How was your day today?

메리 크리스마스! 오늘 어떤 하루를 보냈니?

20

20

20

20

20

What has been the most memorable day of this year so far?

올해 가장 기억에 남는 하루는 언제였어?

20

20

20

20

20

27

Who has had a positive influence on you this year?

올해 나에게 긍정적인 영향을 준 사람은 누구야?

20

20

20

20

20

28

Name three important tasks you need to finish this year.

올해 꼭 마무리해야 하는 일은 어떤 거야?

20

20

20

20

20

29

Write down three big things you must do next year.

내년에 해결해야 할 큰일 세 가지를 적어봐.

20

20

20

20

20

30

What is the luckiest thing that happened to you this year?

올해 가장 운이 좋았다고 생각하는 일은?

20

20

20

20

20

Write down ten items from your bucket list.

너의 버킷리스트 10가지를 써봐.

20

20

20

20

20